To My Darling Daughter

From Your Mother

Presented on This Day

To My Daughter With Love

Loving Thoughts

PUBLICATIONS INTERNATIONAL, LTD.

Louis Weber, C.E.O.
Publications International, Ltd.
7373 North Cicero Avenue
Lincolnwood, Illinois 60646

ISBN: 0-7853-3204-9

Original inspirations by Rebecca Christian

Other inspirations compiled by Kelly Boyer Sagert

Acknowledgements:

The publisher gratefully acknowledges the kind permission granted to reprint the following copyrighted material. Should any copyright holder have been inadvertently omitted, they should apply to the publisher, who will be pleased to credit them in full in any subsequent editions.

Page 41: From *Mothers and Daughters* by Carol Saline and Sharon J. Wohlmuth. Copyright © 1997 by Carol Saline. Photographs copyright © 1997 by Sharon J. Wohlmuth. Used by permission of Doubleday, a division of Bantam Doubleday Dell Publishing Group, Inc.
Page 54: Reprinted from *Mom, You Don't Understand!* by Carol Koffinke and Julie Jordan. Copyright © 1993 by Deaconess Press. Reprinted by permission of Fairview Press.
Pages 72-73: Reprinted from *Mothers & Daughters* by Madeleine L'Engle © 1997 by Crosswicks. Used by permission of Harold Shaw Publishers, Wheaton, IL 60189.

Picture credits:

Front cover: **"Music Room" by Steve Hanks Co.;** Front and back cover background: **Courtesy of the Trustees of The Victoria and Albert Museum/V&A Picture Library/Design by Kate Faulkner for Morris & Co.**

Melinda Byers: 11, 26, 42, 44, 48, 58, 66, 69, 70, 77; **Deborah Chabrian/Artworks:** 47, 52, 61, 62; **Steve Hanks Co.:** Title page, 8, 12, 15, 16, 20, 23, 29, 30, 33, 37, 39, 51, 55, 74; **© Greg Olsen:** "Cream and Sugar" 34, "Denim to Lace" 40, © Greg Olsen by arrangement with Mill Pond Press, Inc., Venice, Florida USA; **Courtesy of the Trustees of The Victoria and Albert Museum/V&A Picture Library/Design by Kate Faulkner for Morris & Co.:** Front and back endsheets.

Original photography by Sacco Productions; Brian Warling.

Contents

Baby Days

There is only one beautiful child in the world and every mother has it.

Anonymous

The moment that I looked into your eyes for the first time was the most memorable moment of my life.

I melt at the sight of a toothless pink smile, a lace bonnet on a downy head.

Susan Lapinski and Michael deCourcy Hinds,
In a Family Way

M. Byers

The most wonderful sound our ears can hear is the sound of a new-born baby.

Unknown

From the moment I first saw your cherubic little face, I had hopes and dreams for you.

Stephanie Pierson, *Because I'm the Mother, That's Why*

Of all the sights that gladden a mother's heart, perhaps the very sweetest is seeing her husband and daughter asleep in a chair, her daughter's downy head warm and heavy on her husband's broad shoulder.

pick up my daughter and
hold her in my arms. Thank you,
God, for letting her be born into
so much love and abundance.

Marianne Williamson, *A Woman's Worth*

"**A**re we there yet?" Often you would ask me that most universal of children's questions in the car. "There" was grandma's house, or the Rocky Mountains, or an amusement park in a nearby town, a glittering place where all would be bright and beautiful and fun.

As I look back, it seems to me we spend much of our lives getting "there." Yet of all the destinations in life, one of the best is a place filled with a daugther's love and laughter. I was "there" the moment you were born. Your baby smiles and gurgles gave me more pleasure than I ever thought possible.

*B*ecoming a mother opened a whole new world of emotions for me. There was that incredible joy when you were first born, a mother tiger's rage when someone hurt you, the almost painful tenderness of watching you asleep or at play. Thank you for enriching my life with the depth of those feelings.

*P*ajamas were soft and warm, grass tickled the feet, soap bubbles had rainbows in them, mashed bananas tasted cool and sweet, and life was grand.

Ann Combs, *We'll Laugh About This...Someday*

*E*very mommy knows that no nonmother or mother-to-be is prepared for how much she will love her baby... once she comes into her life. The feeling is so big and powerful that there are times when it threatens to break your ribs. It preoccupies your thoughts to the exclusion of almost anything else and can make you delirious or absentminded. So essential is that relationship to your well-being that you know that if, God forbid, something were to happen to threaten it, you would disintegrate into a pile of dust.

Vicki Iovine, *The Girlfriends' Guide to Surviving the First Year of Motherhood*

Growing Up

"Just one more!" How often you begged for one more story at bedtime when you were a little girl. And how glad I am now that I usually said yes!

What fun it was to settle
into the lazy rhythm of summer
when you were a little girl.
We played games and went on
outings while the dishes stacked
up in the sink and the grass
grew too high. Supper was when
we got hungry and bedtime was
when we got tired. I miss those
lazy summer days...

Early on, I discovered that the things I'd plan and save for— having your portrait taken, taking you on a nice vacation, getting you the expensive toy that was all the rage that year for Christmas—were fun, but not as much as the simple things. What fun it was just to go out for an ice-cream cone, splash in the backyard wading pool, jump into a pile of bright fall leaves, or hold you tight on a red sled as we flew downhill. Grandma was right, wasn't she? The best things in life are free.

When you were a very little girl, I loved watching you play on the floor and splash in the bathtub and toddle off, unsteady but determined, to explore new worlds. But most of all, I loved watching you sleep—the steady rise and fall of your chest, the slight movement of your eyes under your eyelids as you dreamed, your soft lips just barely parted, exhaling a whisper of air. You were an angel on loan from God.

When springtime comes and
I see the eager yellow beaks of
baby birds stretching up out of
robins' nests, I realize that a theme
runs through all the species:
Mothers love to feed their children.
We had some of our best times
in the kitchen. Your eyes lit up
like sapphires when you
licked the spoon.

"*H*igher, Mommy, higher!"
you would shout when we
went to the park and I stood
behind you, pushing your swing.
All I ever really wanted was for
you to soar up over the rooftops,
following your dreams.
It has given me great pride to
see you fly so high.

When you were small and happily occupied with your toys, I'd steal a few moments to slip away and do something that seemed urgent at the time: phone calls that needed to be made, a house that needed to be cleaned. Now I wish I had spent more time just sitting beside you on the floor, watching your little brow furrow with concentration as you played.

*D*on't you look pretty!
What little girl hasn't grown up
hearing that phrase over and over?
How then can we teach our
daughters that true beauty is not
measured by what we look like on
the outside, but by who we are
inside? That our bodies, however
flawed, are beautiful because
they house our souls.

Carol Saline, *Mothers & Daughters*

When you were a little girl, you loved to play dress up. You'd experiment with my lipstick and costume jewelry, then try on my prettiest bathrobe and pretend you were a princess. The extra fabric pooled behind you on the floor was your train. What mother doesn't love to hear those oh so flattering words, "Mommy, when I grow up, I want to be just like you!"

Becoming Your Own Person

As we crossed each new passage as you were growing up—staying home alone without a babysitter, wearing a little mascara to the mall, expanding the boundaries of where you could ride your bike—I had to admit that you never did belong to me, only to yourself. The joy of seeing you discover who you are has softened the pain of letting you go.

here are many sounds a mother loves to hear from her daughter: the sweet rhythmic sound of her baby's breathing; her toddler's laugh; the teacher's words, "A pleasure to have in class." She loves to hear the phone ring on Sunday when her little girl has moved away. But the sweetest sound is when she hears the car in the driveway (five minutes late) and knows her teenaged daughter has arrived home safely.

*I*f a summer day dawns hot, clear, and windless, I think of other summers, summers with picnics and teddy bear tea parties, fireflies and country drives with you, my bright-eyed companion, singing at my side. I think of you lying on your back in the warm, sweet smelling grass, a dreamy look in your eyes as you watched the clouds roll by. I'm so proud and happy that you are making your dreams come true.

When I first brought you home from the hospital, several mothers advised me, "Enjoy her while you can. She'll grow so fast!" I nodded politely. I was so anxious for all of your milestones—your first smile, your first word, your first step. Then I blinked, and you were setting off for kindergarten. I blinked again, and you were going on your first date. I blinked once more, and you were leaving home. Now I understand the wistful tone those mothers had in their voices.

A daughter notices details. She notices when her mother has tried a new recipe or bought a new tablecloth or planted a rosebush in the side yard. She notices when her brother is trying a new hairstyle or her sister seems a little stressed or her grandmother needs the cheer that a good long visit from her granddaughter brings. A mother sees her daughter noticing. Thank you for being a daughter who sees with her heart.

*D*aughters must try different
pitches to see what song they
want to sing, and what is their best
key. For some, the key of G
may be best; for others,
perhaps the key of C.
A daughter must talk about her
thoughts, feelings, and goals to see
how they fit. She must try a song
to see if it's right. Then she can
throw it out if it's not, but she
won't know before singing it.

Carol Koffinke and daughter Julie Jordan,
Mom, You Don't Understand

*R*emember when we were getting you ready for your first move away from home? Off we went to the discount stores. Marching past pots, pans, TVs, VCRs, answering machines, can openers, bedspreads, wastebaskets, sheets, towels, hot pads. We choose your things from goods piled high in well-lit aisles. The closer the day came for you to leave, the more I bought. "Enough, Mom!" you'd tell me, laughing, "I'll be fine."

What I really wanted to buy you
was a good start on a life of health,
love, laughter, and happiness. What a
joy it turned out to be, seeing you
become independent and realizing that
all along you already had what I was
trying to give you. I couldn't buy you
anything as useful as the resources
you already possessed.

Your Own Family

There are two things you
have to keep in mind when
deciding who to marry: His list
of what's important needs to
be the same as yours, and he has
to make you laugh.

When your own first child comes along, you'll discover that being a mother is like being a Marine: It's the toughest job you'll ever love.

"You never get a second chance
to make a first impression."
"Your eyes will get stuck that way."
"Don't sit so close to the TV."
"Look on the bright side."
"Because I'm the mother,
that's why."
I swore I'd never say the things my
mother said to me . . . until the day
I heard them coming out of my
own mouth. Then I couldn't wait
until I heard you say them!

Reams of advice have been written for mothers. One piece you won't often hear, though, is this: Don't neglect your innermost soul. One of the joys of family is doing for others. I feel so proud when I see you listening, feeding, soothing, cleaning, helping, caring! But oh, my darling daughter, don't forget to do for yourself, too. Take time for a walk in the woods, a half hour in the garden, a manicure, a phone chat with a friend (or your mother!), even a few moments to sip a cup of tea and look out the window. Each day, give yourself permission—however briefly— to restore your soul. For that is what makes the one and only you.

M. Byers

Our Family— Our Strength

Sometimes when you look at me with your beautiful eyes, I see my mother, my grandmother, even myself. And then I understand how mother connects to daughter, all through eternity, time after time.

*O*h my son's my son till he
gets him a wife,
But my daughter's my daughter
all her life.

Dinah Mulock Craik, *Young and Old*

A family is supposed to form a safety net when one of its members is falling. It isn't just there to shine brightly when everything is going perfectly. Family members will have problems from time to time— mom, dad, sisters, and brothers. Drawing on the love, support, and strength of the family can help all of us weather our toughest storms.

Carol Koffinke and daughter Julie Jordan,
Mom, You Don't Understand!

*S*haring can become a wonderful intimacy. Sharing at deep levels, sharing grief, questions about God's love and the world's pain, having private little jokes. Remember the time we put a potato in the muffler of the car so Dad couldn't start it and didn't know we were getting him out of the house to get his surprise birthday party ready?

Remember the time the puppy
unwrapped all the Christmas presents
while we were in church on Christmas
Eve? Remember the time the oven died
on Thanksgiving when we were
expecting twenty people for dinner?
Remember?

Madeleine L'Engle, *Mothers & Daughters*

A Mother's Wisdom

*J*oy is our goal, our destiny.

Marianne Williamson, *A Woman's Worth*

*Y*ou must do the thing you
think you cannot do.

Eleanor Roosevelt

Keep your face to the
sunshine and you cannot see
the shadows.

Helen Keller

Your best teacher is yourself,
and this will always be true.
No one, indeed, can teach you
anything unless you want
to be taught.

Pearl S. Buck, *To My Daughters, With Love*

*W*ith each sunrise,
we start anew.

Unknown

*H*appiness depends
upon ourselves.

Aristotle